Equality and inclusion for learning disability workers

Series Editor: Lesley Barcham

Mandatory unit and Common Induction Standards titles

Communicating effectively with people with a learning disability
ISBN 978 0 85725 510 5

Personal development for learning disability workers
ISBN 978 0 85725 609 6

Equality and inclusion for learning disability workers
ISBN 978 0 85725 514 3

Duty of care for learning disability workers
ISBN 978 0 85725 613 3

Principles of safeguarding and protection for learning disability workers
ISBN 978 0 85725 506 8

Person centred approaches when supporting people with a learning disability
ISBN 978 0 85725 625 6

Equality and inclusion for learning disability workers

Rorie Fulton and Kate Richardson

Supporting the level 2 and 3 Diplomas in
Health and Social Care (learning disability pathway)
and the Common Induction Standards

all about people

Acknowledgements

Photographs from www.crocodilehouse.co.uk and www.careimages.com. Our thanks to Andrew Lee, Our Way Self Advocacy, Sophie and to Choices Housing for their help.

First published in 2011 jointly by Learning Matters Ltd and the British Institute of Learning Disabilities

British Library Cataloguing in Publication Data
A CIP record for this book is available from the British Library

ISBN: 978 0 85725 514 3

This book is also available in the following ebook formats:
Adobe ebook ISBN: 978 0 85725 516 7
EPUB ebook ISBN: 978 0 85725 515 0
Kindle ebook ISBN: 978 0 85725 517 4

Cover design by Pentacor
Text design by Pentacor
Project Management by Deer Park Productions
Typeset by Pantek Arts Ltd
Printed and bound in Great Britain by Ashford Colour Press Ltd, Gosport, Hants

Learning Matters Ltd
20 Cathedral Yard
Exeter
EX1 1HB
Tel: 01392 215560
E-mail: info@learningmatters.co.uk
www.learningmatters.co.uk

BILD
Campion House
Green Street
Kidderminster
Worcestershire
DY10 1JL
Tel: 01562 723010
E-mail: enquiries@bild.org.uk
www.bild.org.uk

Contents

This book covers:

- Common Induction Standards – Standard 4 – Equality and Inclusion
- Level 2 and level 3 diploma units SHC 23 – Introduction to equality and inclusion in health and social care or children's and young people's settings and SHC 33 – Promoting equality and inclusion in health and social care and children's and young people's settings

About the authors and the people who contributed to this book

Crystal

Crystal is 20 years old and lives with her parents. Crystal has drug-resistant polymorphic epilepsy, as a result of which she has severe learning difficulties. However, despite not being able to speak, Crystal is very sociable, as evidenced by the big smiles she gives to all whom she meets. Since leaving school just over a year ago, Crystal attends touch therapy three times a week and dance classes twice a week. Although she would benefit from a wider range of organised activities, Crystal is a very happy person who loves being around others.

Mohammed

Mohammed is a young man who lives with his parents near Cardiff. Mohammed has a learning disability, visual impairment and multiple sclerosis. He really likes going out and about and keeping busy. Visiting Cardiff is one of Mohammad's favourite things, especially going to the library. Mohammed also enjoys being taken to hydrotherapy sessions every week and loves it when his family take him out for meals occasionally. Last but not least, Mohammed is a big fan of rugby – he is passionate about the sport and is a keen supporter of Wales.

Simon and Kimberly

Simon and Kimberly are siblings; they are very sociable and enjoy meeting people. Both Simon and Kimberly have cerebral palsy and mobility difficulties, but despite this they are keen on sports and have done lots of travelling together. Simon and Kimberly were happy to give their time to contribute to this book. They believe a good support worker is one who listens and they hope that by helping with this book they will play a part in helping new support workers to be good listeners.

Akash

Akash is 23 years old and lives at home with his dad and mum in Cardiff. Akash has cerebral palsy and complex health needs. He is a happy, curious and very observant young man. He loves watching people doing things and seeing how things are made or processed. To communicate, Akash makes sounds and eye points to make choices, or points to where he wants to go or what he needs.

During the week, Akash attends a day service and at home enjoys watching his favourite programmes on TV – music channels, nature programmes and game shows. When out and about, Akash enjoys nature walks. His favourite haunt is the Cardiff barrage, where he likes watching the whole process of the working barrage – locks opening and closing and the fishing and leisure boats coming and going.

Kate

Kate is a specialist speech and language therapist working with adults with learning disabilities. Prior to training as a speech and language therapist she worked in the voluntary sector with women from black and minority ethnic (BME) communities and she has experience of advocating for this client group. In addition Kate works as a registered intermediary on behalf of adults with learning disabilities appearing as victims and/or witnesses in the criminal justice system. Kate also works with Rorie running Open Cultures Consultancy, specialising in inclusion, learning disability issues and communication.

Rorie

Rorie is a partner (with Kate) in Open Cultures Consultancy. In addition, Rorie works for a non-governmental organisation supporting asylum seekers and refugees in Wales. He also volunteers for a learning disabilities advocacy service and is a trustee on the board of a mental health advocacy service.

Kate and Rorie are grateful to ABCD Cymru for their support in introducing us to the fantastic contributors we worked with in writing this book. ABCD Cymru work across Wales to support and empower black and minority ethnic children and young people with disabilities and their families to access services. To find out more about ABCD Cymru's work, visit www.abcdcymru.org.uk/

Introduction

Who is this book for?

Equality and Inclusion for Learning Disability Workers is for you if you:

- have a new job working with people with learning disabilities with a support provider or as a personal assistant;

- are a more experienced worker who is studying for a qualification for your own professional development or are seeking more information to improve your practice;

- are a volunteer supporting people with a learning disability;

- are a manager in a service supporting people with a learning disability and you have training or supervisory responsibility for the induction of new workers and the continuous professional development of more experienced staff;

- are a direct payment or personal budget user and are planning the induction or training for your personal assistant.

Links to qualifications and the Common Induction Standards

This book gives you all the information you need to complete both the Common Induction Standard on equality and inclusion, and the unit on promoting equality and inclusion from the level 2 and level 3 diplomas in health and social care. You may use the learning from this unit in a number of ways:

- to help you complete the Common Induction Standards;

- to work towards a full qualification e.g. the level 2 or level 3 diploma in health and social care;

- as learning for the unit on equality and inclusion for your professional development.

This unit is one of the mandatory units that everyone doing the full level 2 and level 3 diploma must study. Although anyone studying for the qualifications will find the book useful, it is particularly helpful for people who support a person with a learning disability. The messages and stories used in this book are from people with a learning disability, family carers and people working with them.

Links to assessment

If you are studying for this unit and want to gain accreditation towards a qualification, first of all you will need to make sure that you are registered with an awarding organisation who offers the qualification. Then you will need to provide a portfolio of evidence for assessment. The person responsible for training within your organisation will advise you about registering with an awarding organisation and give you information about the type of evidence you will need to provide for assessment. You can also get additional information from BILD. For more information about qualifications and assessment, go to the BILD website: www.bild.org.uk/qualifications

How this book is organised

Generally each chapter covers one learning outcome from the qualification unit, and one of the Common Induction Standards. The learning outcomes covered are clearly highlighted at the beginning of each chapter. Each chapter starts with a story from a person with a learning disability or family carer or worker. This introduces the topic and is intended to help you think about the topic from their point of view. Each chapter contains:

 Thinking points – to help you reflect on your practice;

Stories – examples of good support from people with learning disabilities and family carers;

 Activities – for you to use to help you to think about your work with people with learning disabilities;

Key points – a summary of the main messages in that chapter;

References and where to go for more information – useful references to help further study.

At the end of the book there is:

A glossary – explaining specialist language in plain English.

An index – to help you look up a particular topic easily.

Study skills

Studying for a qualification can be very rewarding. However, it can be daunting if you have not studied for a long time, or are wondering how to fit your studies into an already busy life. The BILD website contains lots of advice to help you to study successfully, including information about effective reading, taking notes, organising your time, using the internet for research. For further information, go to www.bild.org.uk/qualifications

Chapter 1

Understanding the importance of diversity, equality and inclusion

Andrew Lee

I think of life as a person with learning difficulties as being taken to watch a football match where life is that football match and never being allowed to join in. People with learning difficulties have the same dreams, inspirations and aspirations as everyone else but we are held back from engaging in life. If you think of your most cherished moments in life, of the things that you still look back on and smile, I expect it is something that people with learning difficulties would get held back from doing. At the root of the barriers we face is an idea that we are less good and less worthwhile than other people.

Andrew Lee, Director, People First Self-Advocacy, from A Life Like Any Other? (2008)

Introduction

Understanding the importance of diversity, equality and inclusion is a key part of supporting people with a learning disability. They are more likely to be discriminated against and often struggle to be part of their wider community. Good support is key to people getting and keeping a job, being happy where they live, seeing family, meeting up with friends and having a relationship. People with learning disabilities often face negative attitudes from society. This chapter provides you with an understanding of why diversity, equality and inclusion are important in social care work and what current good practice is.

Learning outcomes

This chapter looks at:

- what is meant by diversity, equality and inclusion;
- what is meant by discrimination;
- how discrimination may occur and what the effects are;
- how good practice promotes equality, supports diversity and reduces the chances of discrimination happening.

This chapter covers:

- Common Induction Standards – Standard 4 – Equality and inclusion: Learning Outcome 1
- Level 2 SHC 23 – Introduction to equality and inclusion: Learning Outcome 1
- Level 3 SHC 33 – Promote equality and inclusion: Learning Outcome 1

What do we mean by diversity?

The terms 'diversity' and 'equality' do not mean the same thing. Diversity means recognising and valuing individual differences. Equality means recognising differences between groups of people. These differences might be because of age, disability, race, religion, gender or sexual orientation. Recognising diversity means always treating people as individuals. For example, you may be supporting a person with learning disabilities from a

Jewish background and be aware that Judaism does not allow pork and pork products to be eaten. However, arranging with kitchen staff for that person to be given beef instead is of no use if the individual concerned is vegetarian. The same applies if the person is Jewish but they choose to eat pork. So the point is worth making again – diversity means always treating people as individuals, no matter which social group they belong to.

The example above shows how important it is to take the time to find out about the person you are supporting. In your job, valuing diversity means knowing the person you are supporting as an individual, such as their likes, dislikes, wishes and beliefs. This is not always an easy task, and not something that can be done in a few hours. There may be communication issues or you may be supporting someone with profound and multiple learning disabilities. You may need to talk to family members and others who have known the person for a long time. You may need help from an independent advocate to help you to understand the person's needs and wishes.

Whilst many people with learning disabilities may not have their human rights respected, people with profound and multiple learning disabilities are one of the groups most at risk. Other groups at risk are people with learning disabilities whose behaviour is labelled as challenging; people with learning disabilities from black and ethnic minority (BME) communities (who may not have access to information or culturally appropriate support) and people with learning disabilities who are placed in service settings far removed from their families or where they come from. For individuals from these groups, being supported by a learning disability worker who actively and positively values diversity is very important.

Activity

During the next week when you are supporting a person with a learning disability, talk to a colleague about two ways that you can recognise and value individual differences.

People with profound and multiple learning disabilities and complex needs often find it difficult to express their individuality and therefore need more support to do so. This has been recognised in the government's *Valuing People Now* strategy (2009) for England. However, eight years on from the original *Valuing People* White Paper (2001), there is still a gap between what is said in the policy documents and the real experiences of all people with learning disabilities. A recent report into services for adults with profound and multiple learning disabilities found that the major obstacles to implementing

policy for adults with profound and multiple disabilities are *prejudice,
discrimination and low expectations* (*Raising our Sights: Services for adults with
profound intellectual and multiple disabilities*, by Professor Jim Mansell, p.2).
As a learning disability worker, your day-to-day priority is to work against these
negative attitudes. Positively valuing diversity is one of your main tools. You
and your colleagues need to have the hopes, dreams, interests and needs of
each person you support as a top priority in your daily work.

Thinking point

*Imagine someone was supporting you and you were not able to communicate
your choices, in terms of your lifestyle or where you live or simple things like how
you take your tea or coffee. How would you like someone supporting you to get
to know you better? Who would you like them to talk to and how would you like
them to support you?*

What do we mean by equality?

Equality means recognising differences between groups of people. Valuing
equality means recognising that an individual's identity (in terms of their age,
disability, race, religion or belief, gender or sexual orientation) may have an
impact on their life experiences and life chances. By belonging to a particular
social group, for example 'teenage', 'black', 'Muslim', 'traveller' or 'gay', an
individual can become an object of prejudice, discrimination, abuse or worse.
So while an individual's experience of being any of these things may be
positive, it is society's negative attitude or prejudice that can result in negative
life experiences and chances for the individual.

Thinking point

*How would you describe yourself? What makes up your identity? How do you
think other people see you?*

Equality means making sure that people from all social groups – men and
women, people from black and minority ethnic backgrounds, people with
disabilities, older people, people in same-sex relationships and people

of different religions – receive fair and equal treatment. It also means acknowledging that, within an equalities approach, you may need to respond differently to certain individuals or groups. For example, this may mean making sure a person who cannot speak English is helped by an interpreter to access healthcare like any English speaker.

Each of us has prejudices about different groups of people in society. Our prejudices may take the form of assumptions, so that we do not see them as prejudices or ourselves as prejudiced. At some level, each of us has ideas about a certain group or groups in society which, if not all negative, are not all positive. For most of us, most of the time, it is not hard to keep these prejudices in check, assuming we know that we have them. They may be deeply held but are rarely shown in what we say or do. For others it is less easy to control their prejudices. And prejudices can quite easily result in discrimination.

As a learning disability worker, you work with individuals who are some of the most excluded in society. Just because you have chosen to work with people with learning disabilities does not necessarily mean that you are wholly free from prejudice against them. An important part of your role is to be fully aware of your own prejudices. This is called working in a reflective manner – thinking about your own ways of working and checking that you have done all you can to ensure equality of treatment and outcomes for the individuals you support. As part of your commitment to equality, keep in mind the following things.

- You must respect all people with learning disabilities regardless of their age, disability, race, religion, gender or sexual orientation.

- It is important to increase your knowledge and understanding of the person you are working with, especially if their identity is different from your own. You may, without realising it, be having an impact on the person you are working with.

Thinking point

We have all made judgements about others based on stereotypes and negative assumptions. Can you think of a time when you may have treated someone unfairly or did not try to get to know them, based on your negative perception of them?

What do we mean by inclusion?

Inclusion means being included and playing a meaningful part in the life of your community, being a valued and respected member of society. People with learning disabilities can be excluded in a number of ways. In your role as a learning disability worker, it is not enough just to show a positive commitment to diversity and equality. You must promote diversity and equality with a clear understanding of what inclusion is and why it is important in the lives of people with learning disabilities.

Participating in a local election meeting. Inclusion means playing a meaningful part in the life of the community, being able to do the things everyone else does.

Activity

Ask two people where you work about what inclusion means to them. For example, you could ask a work colleague, a person you support or a family carer. Compare their ideas with your own ideas about inclusion and the ideas in this book.

We don't get to meet new people, the only time we can do that is when we take part in the Newport disabled games.

Kimberly, a young woman with learning disabilities whose brother Simon also has learning disabilities.

There are no day services for children when they leave the special school so I had to fight a lot … it was such a draining experience. [Services] would always put the blame somewhere else, it's always like that. It felt like Akash was one of the only people on earth with that need. Staff from the special school feel so sad when the young people leave because they know there won't be anywhere for them to go, they'll just be staying at home.

Mother and primary carer of Akash, a young man with cerebral palsy

Occasionally people are excluded in their family:

> Relatives with disabilities are sometimes 'hidden' away. Mohammed feels that 'my family are not very helpful or supportive' and he is often excluded from family events.
>
> *Support worker to Mohammed, a young man who has learning disabilities, visual impairment, multiple sclerosis and is a wheelchair user*

For people with learning disabilities, inclusion means playing a meaningful part in the life of their community, being a valued and respected member of society. It means being able to do the things everyone else does. Studies show that, for people with learning disabilities, inclusion has two main parts: interaction with others, particularly their friends, family and people in their local community; and access to community facilities and participation in community activities.

As a learning disability worker, you can make a real difference in the lives of the people you support in terms of their inclusion in community life. Remember, people with learning disabilities are some of the most excluded in society, so a small effort from you can make a big difference for them in terms of inclusion. A big effort from you can make a huge difference, a life changing difference. Think for a minute about how important seeing your friends is to you. A survey has shown that 31 per cent of adults with learning disabilities never have any contact with friends. Think of the difference you could make in the lives of the people you support if you make inclusion a central part of your role as a support worker.

Thinking point

Think of a time when you have felt excluded from something. How did it make you feel? Were you able to change your situation or did you need support to do so?

An important part of inclusion for many people with learning disabilities is being given the opportunity and support to form friendships and intimate relationships. Seventy per cent of adults in the general population live as a couple but only 3 per cent of adults with learning disabilities do. However, society is uncomfortable acknowledging the sexuality of people with learning disabilities. Society tends to see people with learning disabilities as needing to be protected from sexual information and relationships. Even people's families sometimes find it hard to recognise the person's desire for close friendships and intimate relationships. But people with learning disabilities have sexual needs and feelings just like anyone else and also the same rights to express these feelings. An important part of your job is to make sure these needs and rights are recognised.

I want to meet other people that are disabled, and then I might get a girlfriend. There aren't many girls to meet and get to know, only my sister.

Simon, a young man with learning disabilities

Here are some tasks that might help social inclusion that you might want to talk to the people you support about and their family carers.

- Make time to just chat with the person you support about anything, rather than just talking about their support needs.
- Support the person you work with to find out about local facilities where they can meet friends or meet new people, for example social clubs, local societies, pubs, youth clubs, cinemas, places of worship, befriending schemes.
- Support the person to visit their families or have their families to visit if they live away from the family home.
- Find out about opportunities for paid work, work placements or volunteering.
- Talk to the person you work with about activities they would like to do in the local area, for example swimming, shopping, going for walks, adult education classes.
- Support them to be able to travel or go out in their local area more independently.
- Support them to phone, text or email their friends and family.
- Talk about social inclusion issues with colleagues in team meetings or one to one supervision.

Activity

Discuss with the person you support, your line manager or the family carer of a person you support about one way that you could promote inclusion in your work.

What do we mean by discrimination?

Discrimination is when someone is not treated well because of the social group they belong to; for example, because of their age, disability, ethnicity, religion or belief, gender or sexual orientation. If someone openly expresses or acts upon prejudices they have about particular social groups then discrimination happens. So discrimination is when one person's prejudice 'comes into the open' and has a negative impact on another person. Discrimination against people with learning disabilities usually involves denying them their rights and the opportunity for inclusion, choice and independence.

A young woman with learning disabilities, Sandra, lives in a residential home. Sandra and Sam, a young man with learning disabilities, decide to date. They see each other regularly at the day centre and feel it is time to meet up just the two of them. They would like to go to a café or to the shops, or perhaps for Sam to visit Sandra at home. She tells him she will telephone him to arrange this. Sandra asks her support workers for help in arranging to meet up with Sam. It is at this point that the potential discrimination begins. Sandra needs support to access and use the telephone and this doesn't happen. Sandra's support workers also use their position wrongly to try to control who she can spend time with and who can come to visit her and spend time alone with her. Despite Sandra often asking for help to meet up with Sam, the support workers keep on finding reasons not to help her arrange a meeting.

What has happened is that Sandra's support workers have chosen to ignore the issue, possibly based on their prejudice against people with learning disabilities having any kind of close friendship or intimate relationship, or maybe their general concern for Sandra's safety. In their concern, or because of their prejudice, Sandra's support workers have discriminated against her by not supporting her to develop her friendship with Sam. They could have raised their concerns with Sandra, her family carers and their manager, also possibly with Sandra's advocate, and explored the issues such as whether she needs some support or advice about intimate relationships or her ability to consent to a sexual relationship. By not supporting Sandra appropriately, the staff have prevented Sandra from possibly developing her relationship with Sam.

Thinking point

What would you have done if you were Sandra's support worker? Do you think you would do anything differently now you know more about diversity, equality and inclusion?

People with learning disabilities experience discrimination in many walks of life, including in:

- education;
- employment;
- housing;
- public places and institutions;
- leisure and recreational activities;
- access to healthcare services.

> Akash having health needs – he was discriminated against in many places where the service wasn't there for him, for example the play scheme – they said it's inclusive, there was an inclusive play scheme but [children with learning disabilities and health needs] were segregated for their own safety.
>
> *Mother and primary carer of Akash, a young man with cerebral palsy*

People with learning disabilities may experience double discrimination because of particular aspects of their identity, for example their ethnicity or gender. People from different ethnic groups often experience racial discrimination on top of discrimination because of their learning disabilities. People with learning disabilities from black and minority ethnic communities can receive insufficient and inappropriate services because of:

- policies and services which are not always culturally sensitive;
- wrong assumptions about what certain ethnic groups value;
- language barriers;
- discrimination.

Women with learning disabilities can also be discriminated against.

- They are often not thought of as reliable witnesses in situations of sexual abuse.
- The parenting skills of mothers with a learning disability are sometimes called into question.
- They have limited access to employment opportunities.

People with learning disabilities can be particularly vulnerable to multiple discrimination. This happens when they are discriminated against because of several aspects of their identity. For example, a woman with learning disabilities might be discriminated against because of her disability but also because of her gender and because she is Pakistani. A man with learning disabilities might come across discrimination because of his disability, but also because he is elderly and from a black African background. Multiple discrimination happens at the same time and the effects of it add up, so that each experience of discrimination reinforces the other.

Thinking point

Have you ever been discriminated against? Why do you think you were discriminated against? How did it make you feel?

Multiple discrimination takes the form of:

- decisions based on negative images of people with learning disabilities;
- restricting people's access to ordinary experiences;
- denying people their rights;
- having low expectations of people;
- interfering in people's personal lives;
- trying to control a person and making their decisions for them.

People with learning disabilities are stigmatised (that is, judged as 'different' by society) and as a result they experience multiple discrimination. The impact on an individual with learning disabilities can include:

- low self-esteem;
- vulnerability;
- low expectations of themselves and of the opportunities available to them;
- poverty and the associated lack of opportunity;
- restricted lifestyles;
- loneliness.

How can deliberate discrimination occur in your work?

Deliberate discrimination can occur when people knowingly ignore legislation or policies that forbid discriminatory practices. This can happen in any number of ways, wherever you support people, for example in their own home, in shared accommodation, a day centre or in their local community. We'll look at deliberate discrimination under the headings:

- how support is provided;
- health needs;
- living environment.

How support is provided

Deliberate discrimination in your work setting is most likely to occur when the model of care (the way the support is provided) is institutionalised rather than person centred. An institutionalised model of care means that the support for people with learning disabilities is based on the convenience of the provider and staffing rotas rather than on the needs of the individuals being supported. Providers may argue that they need to provide support in this way because of lack of funding, low staffing levels and poor training. However, these arguments do not change the fact that support provided according to an institutionalised model of care can lead to deliberate discrimination.

Examples of how deliberate discrimination can occur because of an institutionalised model of care include the following.

- Mealtimes: workers lack specialist training in feeding people with complex swallowing difficulties. The worker feeds the person too quickly to allow for any enjoyment of either their food or the mealtime. The person is not given any choice over what they eat; drinks are only available at certain times. Specific dietary requirements for health or religious reasons are known about, but not met.

- Personal care: a person may receive intimate personal care from a worker of the opposite sex when their support plan says that this is not how they prefer to be supported. The care is provided in a situation where there is a lack of privacy and hence dignity. The person is not involved and there is no meaningful interaction with the individual.

Thinking point

Have you experienced institutionalised care, for example during a stay in hospital? How did it make you feel? Do you recognise elements of the institutionalised model of care in your work setting? How do you think you can change or influence the model of care?

Health needs

Most people with learning disabilities have greater health needs than those with no disabilities. They are also likely to die at a younger age. A number of reports in recent years have shown that there are failings in accessing services and in providing appropriate treatment for people with learning disabilities (*Equal Treatment: Closing the Gap* (2006); *Death by Indifference* (2007)). *A Life Like No Other* (2007), a report into services for people with a learning disability in England, found that adults with a learning disability are particularly vulnerable to breaches of their human rights in healthcare services.

Healthcare workers need specialist training so that they understand about people with learning disabilities and how to communicate effectively.

When people with learning disabilities use health services, staff may have difficulty in meeting their needs because they are unable to communicate effectively with them. Sometimes health professionals are too quick to look at a difficulty a person is having, for example self-injurious behaviour or incontinence, and decide that it is linked to their learning disability, rather than thinking it might be because of other causes such as ill health. In addition, people with learning disabilities may have communication difficulties. It is important to meet the health needs of people with learning disabilities and it is very concerning when they experience discrimination in healthcare settings. This may take various forms.

- People not having annual health checks and a health action plan or being supported to meet their day-to-day healthcare needs.

- A lack of specialist training for healthcare workers so that they understand about people with learning disabilities and how to communicate effectively.

- Failure to assess and meet the needs of people with particular needs such as swallowing difficulties, epilepsy, visual or hearing impairments, obesity, etc.

- Failing to follow medical advice and treatment programmes when they have been agreed.

- A failure by GP surgeries, hospitals and other healthcare providers to make 'reasonable adjustments' in how they provide healthcare support for people with learning disabilities. A reasonable adjustment means changing the way they offer their service so that people with disabilities can access them. This could be by offering a longer appointment, providing information in easy-read formats, etc.

Thinking point

Do you think the person you support receives the same standard of health care as people without disabilities? What would your local doctor, dentist, optician or chiropodist need to do to make their services truly accessible?

Living environment

Deliberate discrimination can occur when too little effort is made to provide a living environment that is either appropriate or homely and comfortable. For example, in a residential home the accommodation may be old and in a poor state of repair or even dangerous and unsafe. Or the home may not meet the person's needs in relation to access or providing enough space if the person uses a wheelchair.

Crystal loves to be with people, she loves to be surrounded with people, she's so happy … she just needs to be occupied; she gets bored so quickly if she's not occupied. So the only thing to do is just put her in the car and drive around or my husband takes her for a walk.

Mother and principal carer of Crystal, a young woman with learning disabilities and severe epilepsy

As we have seen, some people with learning disabilities have few or no friends and little or no interaction with their local community and no job. This can leave large stretches of every day in which they need support to be part of their community or undertake activities they enjoy. An important part of your job is to make sure the person you support has access to activities that are interesting and motivating for them. Discrimination can happen when there aren't enough or appropriate activities for a person to take part in, such as:

- too few activities on offer, so that individuals only get a few hours of activity each week;

- the activities offered are selected by what is available rather than the choices or preferences made by the person with learning disabilities and set out in their person centred plan;

- transport difficulties prevent people going out or to meet friends and family;

- too few staff on duty to take people to do their activities;

- little or no provision of holidays for people with learning disabilities.

Thinking point

Think about what you do in your free time. What kind of things do you enjoy? Do you think the people you support would be able to do the same range of activities you do? How might discrimination prevent them from taking part?

How can discrimination inadvertently occur in your workplace?

Discrimination can inadvertently occur in your workplace because of policies, procedures or a culture which discriminates against people with learning disabilities. This is sometimes called institutional discrimination because in some ways it has more to do with the organisation – its policies, procedures and culture – than with the staff and management of that organisation. Nowadays, the policies and procedures of almost all organisations are inclusive. Institutional or inadvertent discrimination generally happens because of the way the policies and procedures are put into practice – as a result of 'how things are done'. For instance, the policy of an organisation says that it respects and supports people to practise their religious beliefs, but then workers never think about or don't ask the people they support if they would like to go to the church, temple or mosque and the person is not able to practise their faith.

An example of institutional discrimination is when local authorities or support providers fail to promote or offer support to families from a South Asian background. There is a wrong assumption that all people from South Asian backgrounds come from large extended families and that one of the things this family network does is to provide respite breaks. Of course, a person with learning disabilities from a South Asian background may have a large extended family and that family may indeed provide respite breaks. Just as likely, though, the person may have no extended family at all and their family carers may be desperate for respite.

Unless workers ask the people they support about their beliefs, they may not be able to practise their faith.

> There was nobody, we don't have family here. That is what [care services] thought in the beginning, maybe it was a stereotype, they thought I am from an extended family, I will have a family here, because also you will have your community here, but I don't have a community from where I come from [in India].
>
> *Mother and primary carer of Akash, a young man with cerebral palsy*

So whilst the organisation's policy may state that they make respite care available to all, staff on the front line may tend not to offer it to South Asian families based on the wrong assumption that they will not take up the offer or may get offended by the suggestion that they may need respite support.

What are the potential effects of discrimination?

Discrimination can affect people with learning disabilities in a number of ways and on a number of levels. On a practical level, it can mean not being able to find an appropriate place to go to the toilet when out shopping with friends, if they need a Changing Places toilet. It can mean not being able to gain entrance to a building, whether it's the town library or a solicitor's office. Or it can mean not feeling safe when travelling on public transport and so missing out on a special occasion. The public transport may not be adequate:

Mohammed suffers from isolation and exclusion because of inadequate transport services. Buses are infrequent near his home, and he feels trapped. Also, Mohammed feels he doesn't have the same opportunities to travel around the area as other people because of his disabilities. Many buses do not have wheelchair access, and he often finds the drivers are unhelpful or unsympathetic. This makes going out very difficult and stressful for him.

Support worker to Mohammed, a young man who has learning disabilities, visual impairment, and multiple sclerosis and is a wheelchair user

Discrimination can also mean receiving a poor standard of care in hospital, with the result that people experience unnecessary pain or suffering, or even that they die prematurely. The *Death by Indifference* report (2007) and the later investigation *Healthcare for All* (2008) described six stories of people with learning disabilities receiving poor care in NHS and social care settings and dying as a result. Healthcare workers treated people differently because of their learning disability and failed to provide the right treatment.

Discrimination can express itself as abuse or hate crimes. There have been a number of cases in recent years where people with learning disabilities have been exploited, maltreated, abused, tortured and murdered. Such extreme and tragic experiences occur in the community as well as in care settings. More frequent is the day to day name calling and abuse many people with learning disabilities suffer in their own homes, walking down their street and travelling on local buses or trains. Hate crimes are always wrong and often arise out of people's prejudices. As a learning disability worker you need to support people with learning disabilities to get the kind of help they need to report this kind of abuse:

The extent to which society looks down on us contributes to the fact that throughout our lives people with learning difficulties do not get their human rights, and yet there is no public outcry, no-one up in arms about how little choice or control we have over our everyday lives.

Andrew Lee, Director, People First Self-Advocacy, from A Life Like Any Other? (2008)

Principles of Safeguarding and Protection for Learning Disability Workers in this series will help you understand more about reporting abuse.

Discrimination against people with learning disabilities can have an effect on:

- the person with learning disabilities;
- their family and friends.

The potential effects of discrimination on people with learning disabilities

Discrimination can affect how people with learning disabilities feel about themselves and their lives. It can lead to feelings of low self-esteem, low self confidence, anxiety, depression and isolation. It can restrict a person's life experiences and their life chances, allowing them only limited independence and control. In many ways, discrimination can restrict the opportunities that people with learning disabilities have to lead a full and fulfilling life.

Simon: 'She [Kimberly] gets picked on by the blooming kids in the streets when she's on her mobility car, ... They pick on her and touch the machine, ... and they are not supposed to do that at all...' **Kimberly:** 'They don't pick on me now as I don't go out now, I can't be bothered to go out now, I just, I used to go down the road on my own, now I go with Mum ... my chair is battery operated so what they do is they run after it and play with the battery ... So I can get stuck...'

Kimberly and Simon, siblings who both have cerebral palsy

Discrimination means that people with learning disabilities can face difficulties in a number of areas, such as:

- accessing public services, in particular health services;
- not feeling safe when they are out in the community and not feeling confident that the law will defend and protect them;
- not being recognised and treated as equal citizens in society, respected members of their local community whose contribution is recognised and valued;
- not achieving and maintaining an independent life of their own, with the right support;
- not getting paid work;
- not having friends and enjoying a full and varied social life;
- not having relationships and a family.

The potential effects of discrimination on the family and friends of a person with learning disabilities

When a family member has learning disabilities, the impact can be felt by the whole family and relationships with friends and within the community may also be affected:

> My eldest son wouldn't bring his friends home. He didn't tell people about his brother.
>
> My mother-in-law used to phone and ask about each of my other children in turn. I finally asked her why she had not asked about Jane. She told me that she thought I was wrong to keep her at home and that the sooner I put her in an institution the better, before I damaged the other children.
>
> *Mencap, 2001*

When discrimination against the family and friends of a person with learning disabilities happens, it is typically expressed in one of three main ways:

- avoidance (not interacting with someone);
- staring;
- negative comments.

Of these, the most common tends to be avoidance. As a recent survey revealed:

> Parents … find that having a child with autism can impact on how they are perceived socially: people don't invite them to their homes for social occasions, or if they do they don't invite them back. Many are literally shunned by their neighbours, avoided on the streets, and effectively ostracised.
>
> *National Autistic Society, 2007*

Studies have shown that social exclusion is widely experienced by the families of children with disabilities, even to the point of immediate and extended family staying away:

Neither grandparent offered to take Bradley for a walk. My mum used to babysit once in a blue moon, as long as he was in bed. I think it's because they did not accept Bradley as a person in his own right.

My brother was never interested. My mother never bathed her, fed her or babysat for her. They just stayed away because of all sorts of excuses. They never tried.

Mencap, 2001

The experience of social exclusion can be made worse when discrimination takes the form of negative comments, such as the following:

I went shopping in Tesco's and a woman said 'fancy bringing someone like that in here'.

A previous neighbour said that Alison had devalued her property and [she] also called the day centre bus 'the idiot bus'.

Mencap, 2001

The friends of a person with learning disabilities are unlikely to experience the same amount of social exclusion as are the person's family, because they spend less time with them but they too can feel negatively judged even if nothing discriminatory is said or done to them. This experience of being negatively judged is an effect of discrimination.

Thinking point

Considering the examples above, how would you feel if it was someone you loved in this situation? What do you think they could do to change it? As a learning disabilities support worker, what can you do to help educate others in the community?

Promoting equality, supporting diversity and reducing the likelihood of discrimination

People with learning disabilities are discriminated against in society, so part of your job is to help reduce the effects of this on the person you support and also to work to change negative attitudes. You can make a difference by working inclusively.

Here are some practical examples of how you can demonstrate inclusive practice.

- At all times, work in ways that value every individual.

- Listen and support people to express their needs and wants, dreams and aspirations.

- Recognise the adult status of the people you work with and the need to communicate with them at an appropriate level to support their understanding.

One of the ways to work against discrimination is to listen and support people to express their needs and wants, dreams and aspirations.

- Recognise and support a person's racial identity.

- Take full account of age and gender issues in your work.

- Respect each individual and have regard for their dignity and privacy.

- Work in partnership with people with learning disabilities and their family carers to combat discrimination.

- Do not deny a person's learning disability or multiple disability but provide the right level of support so that they can participate in ways and to the extent that they are able.

- Actively promote equality of opportunity in the service and in activities in wider society.

- Have a zero tolerance of all forms of abuse and recognise and address any discriminatory practices or incidents in your work setting.

Activity

Look at the list above and discuss the ideas with your line manager. Identify one or two ways that you could promote inclusion in your work.

There is a lot to do. Of course, nobody expects you to do it all on your own. However, as an individual, never underestimate what you can do towards helping people with learning disabilities achieve their rights. Remember, small acts can have big effects. Let's think about what an inclusive work setting might be like.

Thinking point

Can you think of a time when someone did something quite small for you but which had quite a big effect on you? Why do you think it is that small acts can have big effects?

Advocacy organisations are an important way for people with a learning disability to get together and support each other in speaking up and challenging prejudice and discrimination.

Inclusive practice in your work with people with a learning disability

The best way to support people with learning disabilities to combat discrimination in their lives is by helping them to become empowered. This means helping them to:

- know their rights;
- develop their self confidence;
- gain the self belief to address discrimination.

How far a person is able to do this depends on the extent of their learning disability, as well as their individual situation and opportunities. There will always be people who need others to advocate for them and fight for their rights. But the principle is the same – people with learning disabilities have the right to be recognised as full and equal members of society and to participate according to their own interests and abilities.

Activity

Think of the different parts of your working day. For each part of the day, can you think of two ways in which you can actively empower the person you are supporting? Remember, it doesn't have to be anything big. Discuss your ideas with the person you support or your line manager or the family carer of the person you support.

Advocacy organisations are an important way for people with a learning disability to get together and support each other in speaking up and challenging prejudice and discrimination. As advocacy organisations are mostly independent from support providers, they help people have an independent voice on issues that affect them. Self advocacy is when people speak up for themselves, like Andrew Lee did to the Joint Parliamentary Committee on Human Rights. He is quoted at the beginning of this chapter. Andrew was advocating for himself and other people with a learning disability. Peer and citizen advocacy can support people who are less able to speak up for themselves. As a learning disability worker you could find out details about your local advocacy organisation and help the person you support to access advocacy services. If they want to find their local advocacy service, you should contact the local council or contact the advocacy organisations at the end of this chapter.

If you work directly for a person with a learning disability as a personal assistant or for a really innovative organisation (perhaps one that is run by people with learning disabilities), you will be able to find plenty of opportunities to support people with learning disabilities in their quest for equality and inclusion.

Key points from this chapter

- Positively value diversity in your day-to-day work.

- Make sure people from all social groups receive fair and equal treatment.

- Inclusion means being included and playing a meaningful part in the life of your community.

- Working in an inclusive way can help to reduce the likelihood of discrimination. You can do this by treating each person as an individual, maintaining dignity and privacy, respecting diversity and different cultures and values.

References and where to go for more information

References

Disability Rights Commission (2006) *Equal Treatment: Closing the gap.* London: Disability Rights Commission

Healthcare Commission (2007) *A Life Like No Other?* London: Healthcare Commission

Mansell, J (2010) *Raising our Sights: Services for adults with profound intellectual and multiple disabilities.* Tizard Centre, University of Kent

Mencap (2008) *Death by Indifference.* London: Mencap

Legislation, policies and reports

All UK legislation can be downloaded from www.legislation.gov.uk Policies and reports for Northern Ireland, Scotland and Wales can be found at www.northernireland.gov.uk www.scotland.gov.uk and www.wales.gov.uk respectively. Policies and reports for England can be found on the website of the relevant government department.

Department of Health (2001) *Valuing People: A new strategy for learning disability for the 21st century.* London: Department of Health

Department of Health (2008) *Healthcare for All. Report of the independent inquiry into access to healthcare for people with learning disabilities.* London: Department of Health

Department of Health (2009) *Valuing People Now: A new three year strategy for learning disabilities.* London: Department of Health

Joint Parliamentary Committee on Human Rights (2008) *A Life Like Any Other? Human rights of adults with learning disabilities.* Available at www.parliament.uk

Websites

British Institute of Human Rights www.bihr.org.uk

Changing Places www.changing-places.org

Equality and Human Rights Commission www.equalityhumanrights.com

The Estia Centre www.estiacentre.org

Foundation for People with Learning Disabilities www.learningdisabilities.org.uk

Mencap www.mencap.org.uk

The Norah Fry Centre at the University of Bristol www.bristol.ac.uk/norahfry/

To find an advocacy organisation in England and Wales:

Action for Advocacy www.actionforadvocacy.org.uk

To find an advocacy organisation in Scotland:

Scottish Independent Advocacy Alliance www.siaa.org.uk

In Northern Ireland ask your local council about independent advocacy organisations in your area.

Chapter 2

Working in an inclusive way

Any legislation or procedures brought in to enhance the human rights of adults with a learning disability will only be as effective as the support worker at the sharp end, on duty at that time.

Mencap support worker, in A Life Like Any Other? (2008)

An important part of your responsibility is to make sure that the individuals you support and their family carers understand their rights and can recognise when they are being breached.

Introduction

This Mencap support worker hits the nail on the head. For the person with learning disabilities, all the human rights and equality law designed to promote their welfare and protect them is only as effective as the worker supporting them at the time. So it is up to you, as that support worker, to make sure you know and understand the human rights and equality laws that apply to the work you do and the people you support. An important part of that task is to make sure that the individuals you support and their family carers also know and understand these laws. Too often, people with learning disabilities and their families don't know what their human rights are or when these rights are being breached. Chapter 1 set out why the principles of diversity, equality and inclusion are important in your work. This chapter tells you how to make sure you're putting these principles into practice – that is, how to make sure you work in an inclusive way.

Learning outcomes

This chapter looks at:

- legislation, codes of practice and agreed ways of working (where these apply) that you need to know about in your work role relating to equality, diversity, discrimination and rights;

- working in a way that respects the beliefs, culture, values and preferences of individuals;

- challenging discrimination in a way that promotes positive change.

This chapter covers:

- Common Induction Standards – Standard 4 – Equality and inclusion: Learning Outcome 2

- Level 2 SHC 23 – Introduction to equality and inclusion: Learning Outcome 2

- Level 3 SHC 33 – Promote equality and inclusion: Learning Outcomes 2 and 3.3

Legislation, codes of practice and agreed ways of working

There are three main pieces of legislation and one code of practice you need to know about in your role as a learning disability worker relating to equality, diversity, discrimination and rights:

- the Human Rights Act 1998;

- the Mental Capacity Act 2005 (England and Wales) or the Adults with Incapacity (Scotland) Act 2000;

- the Equality Act 2010;

- the Code of Practice for Social Care Workers.

You will also need to know about the policies and procedures of your organisation that should reflect the legislation. If you work as a personal assistant directly employed by a person with learning disabilities and their family carers, there may not be the policies and procedures that you would find in an organisation. Your contract of employment and the agreed ways of working that your employer discusses with you will form the basis of how you should work. Whatever your work you need to know about these key laws on equality, rights and inclusion and you must work within the law at all times.

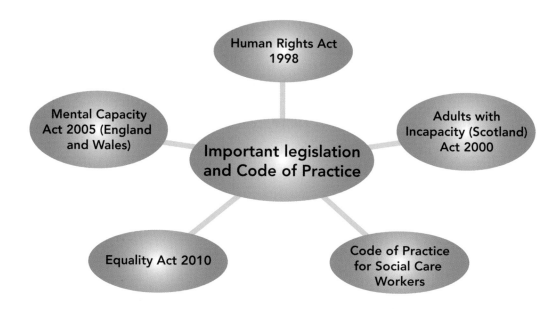

The Human Rights Act 1998

One of the most important laws for you to get to know and understand is the Human Rights Act 1998. Human rights are based on the following core values:

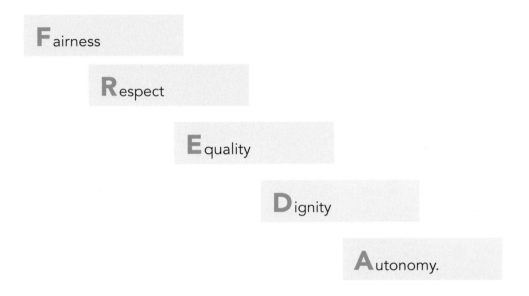

Fairness

Respect

Equality

Dignity

Autonomy.

Activity

Discuss the FREDA values at your next supervision or team meeting. Ask your colleagues how your organisation promotes these values.

These are often called the FREDA values. The Human Rights Act requires public authorities in the UK – including the government, hospitals and social services – to treat people with fairness, equality, dignity and respect. So the Act provides a legal framework within which service providers must operate, and at the same time a legal framework within which individuals can demand to be treated with respect for their dignity. In this way, the Human Rights Act provides each of us with a powerful means of protection against discrimination and injustice. The Act is especially important for people with learning disabilities, who often need support from others to live their lives. The Human Rights Act says that all providers of public services must make sure they do not breach the human rights of people with learning disabilities. Here, 'providers of public services' includes staff in residential homes and day services as well as workers who support people in their own home. An important part of your job is keeping in mind the human rights of the individual you are supporting in everything that you do. You may also need to stand up for their human rights.

Where are disability rights? There are animal rights, where are disability rights?

Mother and principal carer of Crystal, a young woman with learning disabilities and severe epilepsy

All of the rights set out in the Human Rights Act belong to and may apply to people with learning disabilities. The following five rights are often the most relevant:

- the right to not be tortured or treated in an inhuman or degrading way (article 3);
- the right to respect for private and family life, home and correspondence (article 8);
- the right to life (article 2);
- the right to liberty (article 5);
- the right not to be discriminated against (article 14).

The right to not be tortured or treated in an inhuman or degrading way

This right is not just or mainly about torture. The right to not be treated in an inhuman or degrading way is highly relevant to people with learning disabilities.

According to the Human Rights Act:

- inhuman treatment means treatment causing severe mental or physical harm;
- degrading treatment means treatment that is grossly humiliating and undignified.

Only the most serious kinds of mistreatment are covered by this right. Whether or not treatment is inhuman or degrading will depend on the particular circumstances of the case. When the courts decide if the way someone was treated was inhuman or degrading, they will think about lots of things including the person's age, sex, health status and how long this bad treatment went on for. It is important to point out that the treatment does not need to be deliberate – it is the impact it has on the person with learning disabilities that matters. For example, supporting a person to get up, washed and dressed in the morning and not taking account of their dignity and need for privacy.

Organisations, families, learning disability workers and members of the public must actively protect people with learning disabilities from inhuman or degrading treatment. For example, if you know that someone you support is being abused you must do something about it. By not doing something you may be breaching the person's right not to suffer this kind of treatment.

The principle of human dignity is central to the right not to be tortured or treated in an inhuman or degrading way. In your work you may see situations where people are treated in an inhuman or degrading way, for example:

- a person getting bedsores because they are not supported to change position;

- a person being restrained in the wrong way, for example, using force or sedation;

- a person's calls for help being routinely ignored;

- a person being washed or dressed in an undignified way;

- a person who needs help with eating being left with a tray of food in front of them and not given help to eat and drink;

- a person being mimicked or teased or dismissed in an insulting way.

A man with learning disabilities who lived in a residential home became very anxious about bathing after slipping in the bath and injuring himself. So after that, to reassure him and to build his confidence up, a carer, usually female, would sit in the room with him as he bathed. His female carers felt uncomfortable with the arrangement. One carer commented, 'I knew in my heart he was being treated without dignity.' She sought a new care assessment for the man who, in her view, required manual lifting. In the meantime she put up a screen in the bathroom for herself and other carers to sit behind while the man bathed.

From *Your Human Rights: A guide for disabled people, British Institute of Human Rights (2006)*

This example shows how we often know instinctively when an individual's human rights are being breached. It also shows how, even when we try to help someone we can still end up breaching their human rights. If in your work you experience this kind of instinctive feeling that something is not quite right, stop and think for a moment what is going on. Is everything as it should be? Is that individual's right not to be treated in an inhuman or degrading way being upheld? You should discuss your concerns with your manager or employer if you are a personal assistant.

> **Activity**
>
> *Talk to your line manager or your employer if you are a personal assistant. Find out exactly what you should do if you think a person's human rights are being breached.*

The right to respect for private and family life, home and correspondence

On rare occasions, public authorities (e.g. social services) can restrict or limit this right. However, if they do restrict this right they need to be clear why they have done it and it must be lawful, necessary and proportionate. A proportionate restriction is one that is appropriate and not excessive. Organisations supporting people with learning disabilities need not only to respect this right but also to make sure it is respected. For example, social services may need to provide extra support to help a family headed by a person with learning disabilities to stay together.

Respect for family life

Family life does not just mean blood relatives; it also covers close and personal ties of a family kind. The right to respect for family life includes being able to live together and, in situations where this is not possible, having regular contact. This right is important for people with learning disabilities, especially if there is a risk they will be separated from their partner, children or other family members, or are at risk of having very limited contact with them. Just the idea of being separated from their parents, partner or children is enough to fill most people with dread and horror. Yet this is by no means an unusual experience for people with learning disabilities. Families that include a person with a learning disability may also face unnecessary intrusion or feel overwhelmed by their responsibilities, which can destroy family life.

A number of reasons are given for separating people with learning disabilities from their family. People with learning disabilities may be placed in residential accommodation far from home and family; this makes it difficult for them to stay in contact:

Mohammed has communication problems and struggles with his speech. This causes him to feel isolated as it can be hard to connect and communicate with people. The problems he experiences with isolation were made worse when he was accommodated far away from his family. Then he was sent from South Wales to a respite centre in Liverpool. Mohammed said: 'I felt alone in Liverpool. I didn't like it there.' His loneliness was made worse because most of the people there were elderly, and he was the only young person. There was a 'one size fits all' approach taken to disabled people.

Support worker to Mohammed, a young man who has learning disabilities and complex needs

In some circumstances a local authority may have a concern about whether a person with learning disability is able to be a good parent to their child. These are complex situations as those working with the person need to balance the rights of the parent and the rights of the child. Your job may involve supporting a person with learning disabilities to be able to stay with or near their family or to look after and bring up their own children. Remember, it is their human right to do so, and any restriction on this must be lawful, necessary and proportionate.

Respect for private life

The Human Rights Act defines 'private life' broadly. Private life is not just about privacy, it includes things such as:

- being able to live your personal life as you choose;
- being able to form relationships with others as you wish;
- being able to take part in the life of the community;
- your physical and mental wellbeing;
- having access to your personal information, e.g. medical or financial records;
- having personal information about your private life kept confidential.

For people with learning disabilities, because they often rely on the support of other people to live their lives, the right to respect for private life can be especially important. It includes a right to personal autonomy – making their own choices about their life and having support with this – and human dignity. For people with learning disabilities, the right to respect for their private life may be particularly relevant in the following respects:

- *Privacy concerning their body*: who sees and touches your body is a fundamental part of private life.

- *Personal and sexual relationships*: people with learning disabilities have the same right as anyone to have relationships.

- *Taking part in community life*: this means being able to enjoy the same access to work, social, cultural and recreational activities as everyone else.

- *Abortion*: a woman with learning disabilities has the right to make her own choices about whether or not to keep her baby, unless she lacks capacity to make this decision.

- *Decisions about treatment*: provided a person with learning disabilities has the legal capacity to make a decision about a particular treatment, then they have the right to decide whether to go ahead with medical treatment.

An important part of your job is helping the person you support to understand their human rights and to support them to know when their rights are being breached or are at risk of being breached. You can do this by using accessible materials, DVDs and giving the person information about local advocacy services if they don't already have them. An equally important part of your job is to do all you can to uphold that person's human rights if they are at risk of being breached.

Activity

Can you think of any ways in which a person you support does not have their private life respected? What steps could you take to ensure their private life is respected? Discuss your ideas with your manager at your next supervision.

Respect for home

This is not a right to housing but rather a right to respect for the home you already have. For people with learning disabilities, this right can be especially important if circumstances mean they have to leave their own home. In order to ensure respect for a person with learning disabilities' right to their home, public authorities must take their needs into account and any action taken must be justified as lawful, necessary and proportionate. In your role as a learning disability worker, it is important that you support the person to have their voice heard and their needs recognised. Using person centred approaches and planning are particularly important in such a situation. Make sure the person has a person centred assessment that identifies their support needs and ways to address them.

The right to life

This says that public authorities:

- *must not take away a person's life* except in a few very limited circumstances;
- *must take reasonable steps to protect a person's life.*

The duty to protect life does not mean that everything possible must always be done to save life. Sometimes helping someone to live longer means they suffer so much it is not fair to keep trying to save their life. As long as the person has capacity (that is, they are able to make a decision for themselves at the time when the decision needs to be made), the person must give consent (agree) before they are allowed to die. As a learning disability worker you may be involved in issues relating to the right to life when you are supporting a person who is seriously ill or when consent to treatment is needed. You will need to work closely with other people to support the person in such situations, such as their family and friends, their doctor and other medical staff, and their advocate. Your organisation's policies and procedures will explain what you should do.

The right not to be discriminated against

This is discrimination that happens when a person with learning disabilities can show that they have been treated in a different way compared with someone else in a similar position.

> A 26-year-old woman had a 50 per cent chance of surviving the cancer with which she had been diagnosed. However, hospital staff were worried that the woman's learning disability would make her difficult to treat, so they decided not to treat her. When the woman's mother asked one of the doctors what would have happened if her daughter hadn't had learning disabilities, she was told that treatment for the cancer would have begun immediately.
>
> From BBC news report, *Learning disabled care is 'worse'*, 20 June 2010, available at: www.bbc.co.uk

Sadly, this kind of discrimination is not uncommon, indeed NHS staff themselves recognise it. Recent research by Mencap shows that 40 per cent of doctors and 33 per cent of nurses think that people with learning disabilities are discriminated against in the NHS, whilst 45 per cent of doctors and 33 per cent of nurses have actually seen a patient with learning disabilities being neglected or denied their dignity. It is important for you to be aware of this when you support someone to access health care and to support them appropriately and effectively if they are discriminated against.

Thinking point

Can you think of a time when you accompanied a person with learning disabilities to a healthcare setting? What did you think about the way they were treated by healthcare staff? Could anything have been done differently or better?

Activity

Familiarising yourself with the Human Rights Act

Use the internet or a library to familiarise yourself with the Human Rights Act and find out more about how it relates to the lives of people with learning disabilities. At a supervision or team meeting, share what you find out.

The Mental Capacity Act 2005

The Mental Capacity Act is an important law for people with learning disabilities in England and Wales and one that you need to know and understand clearly if you are to support people with learning disabilities effectively. In Scotland the relevant law is the Adults with Incapacity (Scotland) Act 2000; in Northern Ireland mental health issues are currently dealt with under common law although there are plans to introduce capacity legislation. The Mental Capacity Act provides a legal framework for acting and making decisions for people aged 16 or over who are unable to make such decisions themselves. The kind of decisions the Mental Capacity Act covers includes decisions relating to health, welfare, finance and property.

The Mental Capacity Act says that people have capacity unless it can be shown that they cannot make their own decisions. This is important for people with learning disabilities because people often presume they do not have capacity.

It should be assumed that an adult (aged 16 or over) has full legal capacity to make decisions for themselves (the right to autonomy) unless it can be shown that they lack capacity to make a decision for themselves at the time that the decision needs to be made.

Mental Capacity Act 2005, Code of Practice 1.2

The Mental Capacity Act also says that an individual can only be treated as unable to make a decision if all practical steps to help them make the decision have been taken. When the person is judged to lack capacity to make that particular decision, the decision which is made for them must be made in their best interests and also be made in a way that is least restricting of their rights and freedom of action.

Some individuals who lack capacity may also have no family or friends who would be appropriate to talk to about important decisions. When certain types of decision are being made, NHS services and local authorities must make sure that an advocate is appointed to represent and support the person. An advocate is an independent person who can speak up for an individual with learning disabilities or help them to speak up for themselves. This includes decisions about:

- serious medical treatment;
- changes of accommodation;
- care reviews;
- adult protection cases.

The important things for you to remember about the law and capacity issues are:

- all adults are presumed to have capacity to make decisions;
- a person may only be treated as unable to make a decision if all practical steps to help them make the decision have been taken;
- any decision made on the person's behalf must be made in their best interests after a sharing of views by people who know the person well, for example their family and friends, or workers who have known them a long time;
- any decision made on the person's behalf must be made in a way that is least restricting of their rights and freedom of action;
- a person who lacks capacity and also has no family or friends who would be appropriate to ask about important decisions should be represented and supported by an advocate.

For more information about supporting people to make decisions about treatment, see the BILD book *A Brief Guide to the Mental Capacity Act 2005: Implications for people with learning disabilities* by Elaine Hardie and Liz Brooks.

Activity

Familiarising yourself with the capacity legislation in your country

Use the internet or a local library to familiarise yourself with the Mental Capacity Act or the relevant law/s in your country and find out more about how it relates to the lives of the people with learning disabilities you support. Or go on a training day about capacity issues. At a supervision or team meeting, share what you find out.

Supporting people to make choices in their day-to-day life is a practical way that you can work with people so that they are used to making decisions about their life, and this includes:

Support people to make choices in their daily life, by making information accessible.

- working in a person centred way and respecting people's individuality and choices;

- offering choices in everyday situations and respecting the person's decisions and acting on them;

- making information about possible choices available in accessible ways for the person you support. This could be using pictures, signs or easy-read materials;

- knowing the best time and place to discuss options and alternatives;

- checking the person's decision at a later time, giving them time to change their mind or opt for an alternative;

- recording the person's decisions.

Activity

Find out from your line manager about the arrangements in your organisation for supporting people with decision making and for assessing capacity. Also find out how family carers are involved and have access to information so that they can be supported if they are partners in making a best interest decision.

The Equality Act 2010

The Equality Act 2010 brings together under one law all previous laws about discrimination in Britain (in Northern Ireland, which is not covered by the Equality Act, people will have different protection against unlawful discrimination, harassment and victimisation until the law there is changed). The Equality Act provides legal protection against discrimination under six main equality 'strands'.

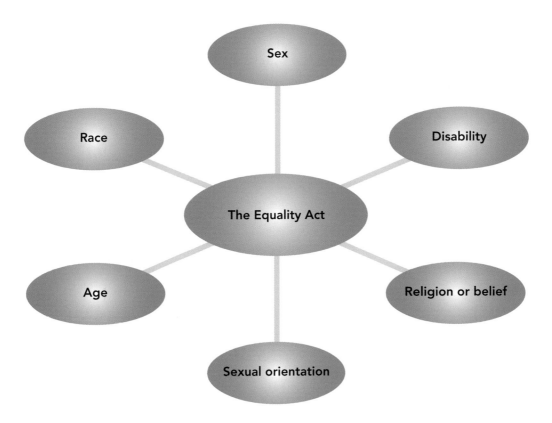

The six main equality strands are:

- sex;
- race;
- disability;
- age;
- religion or belief;
- sexual orientation.

In terms of disability discrimination, the Equality Act 2010 replaces the Disability Discrimination Acts 1995 and 2005. For people with learning disabilities and those who support them, the Act also introduces some changes.

- It protects a person from being discriminated against because they are linked or associated with a person with disabilities. This new protection could be important for family carers and for you as a learning disability worker. It makes it unlawful for a business or service provider to discriminate against a family carer or you because you are with or associated with a person or people with learning disabilities.

- Direct discrimination against people with disabilities is now unlawful not only in the workplace but when individuals are accessing goods and services. For example, a pub or restaurant cannot refuse to serve a person because they may need support to eat.

- It is unlawful to discriminate against an individual because of something connected with their disability. This is called discrimination arising from disability. An example would be telling a man with a hearing impairment that he cannot stay in a hotel because he would not be able to hear the fire alarm.

- It is now unlawful to cause indirect discrimination. This is when there is a rule, policy or even practice that is for everyone, but that makes things harder for people with a disability.

- Disability harassment is now unlawful. This is when someone's behaviour violates a person with a disability's dignity or creates an environment for them that is intimidating, hostile, degrading, humiliating or offensive. For example, calling someone with a disability names or bullying them because they have a disability.

The Social Care Councils' Code of Practice for Social Care Workers

The social care councils for each of the four countries of the UK (for details see the end of this chapter) were set up by the UK government in 2001 to register and regulate social workers and social care workers. Each council has set out in a Code of Practice the standards which all social care workers in that country must work to. The four codes each have six similar standards which describe the conduct that is expected of social care workers. It says that social care workers must:

1. protect the rights and promote the interests of service users and carers;
2. strive to establish and maintain the trust and confidence of service users and carers;
3. promote the independence of service users while protecting them as far as possible from danger or harm;
4. respect the rights of service users whilst seeking to ensure that their behaviour does not harm themselves or other people;
5. uphold public trust and confidence in social care services;
6. be accountable for the quality of their work and take responsibility for maintaining and improving their knowledge and skills.

Each section includes a number of statements which describe in more detail what exactly is expected of the social care worker. It is important that you familiarise yourself with the Code of Practice for the country you work in and that you work to the six standards. The social care council in your country may take action against you if you fail to do so. Also, you should use the Code to reflect on how you work and to look for areas where you could improve. Remember, your employer will take account of the standards set out in the Code of Practice in considering issues of misconduct. The Codes of Practice will undoubtedly be similar to your own organisation's policies, but the difference is they are set at a national level and have been written to make sure people who are supported, their families, carers and other members of the public know the standards of conduct they should expect from social care workers.

Activity

Find and read the Code of Practice for the country that you work in. Talk to your line manager or employer about how as a social care worker you protect the rights and interests of the people you support and their family carers.

Organisational policies and procedures

When you start a new job, you should receive induction training during which you are made aware of all your organisation's policies and procedures. If you work as a personal assistant you too should receive induction training and you should find out from your employer whether they have policies and procedures for their staff or if they have agreed the ways that you should support them, e.g. though a contract of employment or supervision.

Wherever you work, your induction is the time when you need to make sure you properly understand your role and responsibilities, especially in terms of what to do and who to go to if you have concerns about the rights of the person you support. If you feel you do not understand the policies and procedures, or agreed ways of working, or you need more information about your role and responsibilities, talk to your line manager about it in supervision. Don't be afraid to ask questions, as it is important you know and understand what to do if you have concerns.

Working in a way that respects the beliefs, culture, values and preferences of individuals

As a learning disability worker you must actively support the values of respect, independence, individuality and personal choice. In order to do this well and in a person centred way you will need to understand the person you work with, their beliefs, culture, values and preferences. Understanding and respecting people's background and how it might affect the support you provide is all about respecting diversity and working in an inclusive way. It is important to understand that without active support many expressions of diversity, such as keeping up special days of celebration, will simply fade away.

There may well be people with learning disabilities you support who are from different backgrounds to your own. This means that their and their family's understanding of care and support services may differ from yours. For example, you might work with people from cultural backgrounds who:

- live very closely with extended family members;
- have lots more people in their close family;
- have particular family traditions;
- have different expectations of the role of men and women;
- have different marriage practices;
- have different ideas of what ability and disability mean;
- expect sons and daughters to live with the family until marriage;
- have important religious requirements;
- have particular dietary requirements;
- have particular preferences in relation to their daily routine and personal care.

Different cultural backgrounds

Think about how you could find out about the cultural background of a new person you are supporting. How could you find out about their values and beliefs? Discuss your ideas with your line manager or a senior colleague.

There are many practical ways that support workers and organisations can show people that their cultures and values are respected.

- When working with a person to write their support plans or person centred plans, asking whether information on the person's ethnic and religious background is helpful to include.

- Encouraging all new workers to read the person's support plan. When a service supports someone from a different ethnic or religious background from most of the staff, it is helpful if someone from a similar background is involved. If you are not sure about how to support the person always ask – you can ask the person, members of their family, their advocate, community or religious leaders from their community, friends who know the person well.

- Incidents of racism, ageism and sexism should be challenged and managed appropriately by all the support workers in an organisation whether the discrimination comes from members of the public or employees.

- The culture and traditions of people and their families should be respected and observed. Practical arrangements can be made to support important practices relating to food, religion, personal care and significant events.

There are many ways that support workers can show people that their cultures and values are respected.

Activity

Respecting culture and values

Write down three practical ways that you can show respect for a person's culture and values. Discuss your ideas with your line manager.

As you can see, getting into the habit of thinking about how you can promote diversity and support different cultures and values is important for learning disability workers.

Challenging discrimination in a way that promotes positive change

Challenging discrimination can be difficult. Imagine you are queuing at the post office waiting to be served when the man in front of you makes a racist comment about the cashier, who he thinks is being too slow. The racist comment is deliberately loud enough to be heard by the other people in the queue and the man who makes it seems to expect that everyone will agree with him. It is also loud enough to be heard by the cashier. What do you do? If you are going to challenge the man's discriminatory comment, you have to do it quickly, or the opportunity will be lost. By far the easiest option for you, as a bystander, is to say and do nothing. Indeed, this may be your instinctive response. You might say to yourself, *I can't believe he just said that! Next time I hear anyone say something like that, I'll definitely challenge them.* And you might exchange a glance with the person behind you in the queue as if to say, *Can you believe he just said that? Some people!*

Reacting like this, you maintain your self-image as someone with principles, someone who cares about people from ethnic minorities and is prepared to stand up for them (next time). But reacting like this, you change nothing and you risk nothing. Challenging discrimination can be a risky business. By challenging the man who made the racist comment, you take a number of risks. For example:

- the man may verbally or physically abuse you;

- the other people in the queue may side with the man and abuse you;

- the cashier may resent your intervention and prefer for the racist comment to go unchallenged.

When we witness someone being discriminated against, there are different ways we can respond.

- A purely instinctive response is that we challenge the discrimination almost as soon as it has happened because it offends our ideas about what is fair and right. However, this is unlikely to promote positive change, not for the person discriminated against, not for the person discriminating, and not for any observers. It can lead to confrontation and end up, possibly confirming the racist (or sexist, or homophobe…) in their views.

- Another way to respond is to begin with some kind of questioning; for example, you might ask the man in the queue, *How do you think the cashier feels about your comment? I found your comment to be discriminatory; can you understand why?* This kind of challenge is non-confrontational and hopefully it will start a dialogue and give an opportunity to discuss discrimination.

In the course of your work, you may see people saying or doing discriminatory things – a colleague, a senior manager, even a person with learning disabilities or a member of their family. Your instinct may be to turn a blind eye or to play the incident down in your mind, telling yourself it wasn't actually as bad as it seemed. However, as a learning disability worker it is your duty to stand up for the rights of the person your support. These practical suggestions may help you think through how you might respond to a discriminatory action.

- Consider when it might be best to intervene, but remember, saying nothing may be seen as accepting the discriminatory behaviour.
- Avoid acting in an aggressive, confrontational or judgemental way.
- Ask the person what the impact of their words or actions might be on the individual they are discriminating against.
- Support the person to complain if they are discriminated against.
- Talk through with your line manager or an experienced colleague how you might respond.

Also by promoting diversity, equality and inclusion and working in a person centred way you can demonstrate how to work in a non-discriminatory way by discussing human rights and equality with the people you support, their family carers and your colleagues. This also raises awareness.

Thinking point

What would you have done if you'd been in the queue in that post office? Have you ever been in a similar situation? How did you respond? Could you have responded differently?

Key points from this chapter

- The Human Rights Act is based on the FREDA values of fairness, respect, equality, dignity and autonomy.

- It is important for support workers and people with learning disabilities and their family carers to know about human rights.

- The Equality Act 2010 replaces the earlier legislation on disability discrimination.

- It is important to remember that laws on capacity assume that all adults are presumed to have capacity to make decisions.

- The Code of Practice for Social Care Workers, first standard, says that a support worker must protect the rights and promote the interests of people who use support and family carers.

References and where to go for more information

References

Code of Practice for Social Care Workers, available at:

General Social Care Council (England) www.gscc.org.uk

Care Council for Wales www.ccwales.org.uk

Northern Ireland Social Care Council www.niscc.info

Scottish Social Services Council www.sssc.uk.com

Hardie, E and Brooks, L (2009) *Brief Guide to the Mental Capacity Act 2005. Implications for people with learning disabilities.* Kidderminster: BILD Publications

Ministry of Justice (2008) *A Guide to the Human Rights Act: A booklet for people with learning disabilities.* Available at www.justice.gov.uk

Legislation, policies and reports

All UK legislation can be downloaded from www.legislation.gov.uk

Policies and reports for Northern Ireland, Scotland and Wales can be found at www.northernireland.gov.uk www.scotland.gov.uk and www.wales.gov.uk

respectively. Policies and reports for England can be found on the website of the relevant government department.

Human Rights Act 1998

Adults with Incapacity (Scotland) Act 2000

Mental Capacity Act 2005

Equality Act 2010

Northern Ireland: mental capacity issues are currently dealt with under common law although there are plans to introduce capacity legislation.

Websites

About Learning Disabilities www.aboutlearningdisabilities.co.uk

British Institute of Human Rights www.bihr.org.uk

British Institute of Learning Disabilities (BILD) www.bild.org.uk

Equality and Human Rights Commission www.equalityhumanrights.com

Chapter 3

Accessing information to promote diversity, equality and inclusion

> We need to remember that we are talking about people who on the whole have not only had their rights denied for centuries, but have actually lived in an environment where they have been taught not to have great expectations in life.
>
> *Rob Greig, National Co-Director for Learning Disabilities, from A Life Like Any Other? (2008)*

Despite changes in law and policies in recent times, the historical exclusion of people with learning disabilities continues today. Sometimes it is clearer to see, for example in accounts of disability hate crime or the fact that so few people with learning disabilities have jobs. Sometimes the exclusion is harder to see, for example, people with learning disabilities having low expectations of themselves, reflecting society's low expectations of them.

In your role as a learning disability worker, it is important that you promote the principles of diversity, equality and inclusion. You need to promote these rights to the people you support and your colleagues, as well as people who might discriminate against those with learning disabilities. Remember that many people with learning disabilities are vulnerable but that certain groups are especially vulnerable. So you need to get to know where to go to find different sorts of information for different groups of people. For example, you may be asked to support an individual from a black or minority ethnic community, an individual described as having challenging behaviour, an individual with complex needs or an individual who prefers same sex relationships. And of course you yourself also need to know whom to ask for support about diversity, equality and inclusion. This chapter tells you all about promoting and accessing the information, advice and support you need.

Situations in which additional information, advice and support may be needed

People with learning disabilities have the same human rights as anyone else – they have the right to as full and varied a life as anyone else. If, when you are working with someone and you feel they are not able to live a full and varied life like people without a learning disability, it may be a time when you need to get extra information or advice about diversity, equality or inclusion.

Activity

Think about the example in Chapter 1 about Kimberly no longer going out on her mobility scooter because of harassment from young people in her street. Can we say she is living her life to the fullest? Is she being restricted in her freedom and choices? Talk to your colleagues about what you would do if you were her support worker. Find out where you would go to get extra help and advice to support Kimberly.

The things you need extra information, advice or support with will vary. They could be related to serious issues such as abuse or more everyday issues such as choice over activities.

Before we consider these different kinds of situations, let's first of all think about the different kinds of people you might be supporting.

The things you need extra information, support or advice with will vary. They could be related to serious issues such as abuse or more everyday issues such as choice over activities.

Thinking point

How well do you know the person you are supporting? What have you done to get to know the person?

Valuing diversity is important to help you to get to know the person you are working with. The more you know about the person you are supporting, the better you will be able to support them. Knowing them helps you to understand their individual needs and preferences and helps you to know what extra information, advice and support you may need to support them. In these situations you may need additional information.

- *Supporting a person of the opposite sex.* Supporting a person of the opposite sex may mean you need to find out more information about diversity, equality and inclusion. It is important you know how to support them with issues relating to sexual health and gender specific issues, for example particular health checks for men or women, contraception, pregnancy and childbirth.

- *Supporting a person from a different ethnic group.* If the person you're supporting is from a different ethnic group, you need to find out more about that group whilst remembering what we have learnt about diversity – everyone is different, we are all individuals. One thing that unites people from a minority group is their experience of being from a minority (a smaller group within society) and possibly their experience of racism. Remember also that the person you are supporting has a learning disability, which means they belong to another minority group.

- *Supporting a person from a different cultural background:* Culture is difficult to define but basically we can say that it's when a particular group of people share certain beliefs, expectations and ways of doing things. Often, a group of people may share the same religion or come from the same part of the world, or both. Culture can also be defined by a

You need to be open and learn about cultural differences to make sure you are supporting the person with a learning disability in a truly person centred way.

group's disabilities, for example in the case of Deaf culture. Inevitably, when we talk about cultural background, we often have to generalise – to talk about that cultural group as if all of its members share the same beliefs and do things in the same way, when clearly they don't (diversity again!).

Cultural differences exist and you need to be aware of possible difference and be ready to be open and learn about cultural differences to make sure you are supporting the person with a learning disability in a truly person centred way. For instance, if the person you're supporting is from a black African or Asian community, things like diet, dress and religious practices may be important in the support you provide. However, it is important to remember that this may not be so; the best thing to do is ask them or their family, friends, an advocate or a support worker from the same community. It is also good to remember that people can have lots of different cultural identities, for example British, British Asian, Hindu, Deaf, etc. So this comes back to diversity, and getting to know the person as an individual. It is important to remember that the model of care is historically based on 'English' traditions that may not fit with the cultural needs or preferences of people from a different cultural background. So don't forget to recognise that anything you do will be influenced by your own cultural background and the fact that care models are not free from cultural influence. Learning about someone's cultural needs and preferences will make you better at your job and your relationship with the person you support will grow.

- *Supporting a younger or older person:* If you are asked to support an individual who is much older or younger than you, it is worth finding out about the kinds of challenges and opportunities they might encounter as an older or younger person. For example, an older person's health needs may be different to those with which you are familiar. If the person you are supporting is much younger than you, there are other things you'll need to find out about. These may have to do with, for example, facilitating access to different types of social networking such as Facebook, YouTube or Twitter. It is important to understand the person's needs and preferences, for example, what kind of music they like, what type of clothes, activities or television programmes.

- *Supporting a person who prefers same sex relationships.* A person with learning disabilities who prefers same sex relationships may need quite specific kinds of support from you. It is important that you get appropriate advice if you are unsure how best to support a person to access information or support about sexuality and relationships. As a starting point, an easy-read resource on same-sex relationships on the Scottish Independent Advocacy Alliance website might be helpful. If the person you are supporting can access the local community team for people with learning disabilities, a referral to the team may help you to provide the best advice and support you can.

- *Supporting a person with different religious beliefs or no belief.* If the person you're supporting has different religious beliefs to your own, you will be able to support them more effectively if you have found out about their religion and the practices and special days that go with it. You may need to know, for example, about special dietary requirements, personal care needs and dress codes. Equally, if the person you're supporting has no religious beliefs, they may prefer, for example, not to attend a religious event such as a Christmas carol service.

- *Supporting a person described as having challenging behaviour.* This may take the form of aggression, self-injurious or stereotyped behaviour or withdrawn behaviour that significantly affects the person's quality of life. It is recognised that these behaviours are not under the control of the individual concerned and can often be due to the individual's communication needs not being met. So to provide effective support to a person described as having challenging behaviour, you need to make sure you have done all you can to support their communication. You may need specialist advice and support to do this, and your local speech and language therapy department or positive behaviour support team in the local community team for people with learning disabilities may be able to help. You may also need additional communication training, for example in Total Communication, Makaton, Signalong or Intensive Interaction. It is worth talking to your line manager about any training needs you have. The internet is a good place to go for information. The Challenging Behaviour Foundation provides a range of resources to help you support a person described as having challenging behaviour: www.thecbf.org.uk

- *Supporting a person with a specific learning disability condition or syndrome or with profound and complex needs.* Some people with learning disabilities have a specific condition or syndrome that might include a particular impairment or need. Or the person you support may have a learning disability as well as other physical or sensory impairments. For example, some individuals with autistic spectrum condition typically benefit from having a structured routine and a predictable environment. People with Down's syndrome have a higher risk of having hearing impairment than the general population. Learning about different conditions and syndromes helps you understand what extra support someone may need.

In addition to knowing the person you are supporting, you need to know a bit about the local area so that you can support the person to access the community and take part in activities that interest them, volunteer or find work locally. Some good places for you to go with the person you support to find local information include the library, town hall, community centre, local shop or pub, the volunteering service or supported employment organisation.

It is important to know the local area and the opportunities there are for the person you are supporting to help them to become involved in the life of the community.

Thinking point

How well do you know the local area where the person you are supporting lives?

It is important to know the local area and the opportunities there are for the person you are supporting to help them to become involved in the life of the community. You will need to be proactive in the way you provide support, in making links and building relationships with local organisations or groups and in creating opportunities for inclusion. You won't know if you need extra information about inclusion until you know what's out there and what's not.

In addition to needing extra information, advice and support to help you get to know the person you are supporting, you also need to recognise situations where you need extra information or support.

Situations in which you might need extra information, advice or support include when the person you're supporting:

- is about to move house;

- needs to access health care or go to hospital;

- wants access to education or training;

- has additional communication needs;

- wants to find a job;

- needs extra assistance to be able to undertake the activities of daily living as independently as possible such as eating, dressing, getting into or out of bed, taking a bath or shower and using the toilet;

- needs access to meaningful daily activities;

- has restricted choices;

- if you think that someone is being harassed or is at risk of being a victim of hate crime.

Early signs of disability hate crime include persistent vandalism of an individual's property or home, whispering campaigns, graffiti, verbal or physical harassment and theft, typically of money or medication. For more information on recognising and responding to abuse, read *Principles of Safeguarding and Protection for Learning Disability Workers* in this series.

How to access information, advice and support about diversity, equality and inclusion

If a situation arises where you need to get extra information, advice or support, it is important you know who to talk to or where to go. The resources available to you come under the four main headings:

- the internet or local library;

- your work setting;

- the statutory sector (government or local authority organisations, for example the National Health Service or Adult Social Services);

- the voluntary sector (charities and voluntary organisations such as the Citizens Advice Bureau or Mencap or The PMLD Network).

The internet or local library

The internet is an invaluable tool for accessing extra information. Simply inputting a question or phrase into an internet search engine can often provide very useful results, although you need to be careful about where you source your information from. Not everything you find on the internet is correct. You can get information from the main national and local government websites such as the NHS, your local council, the Department of Health, Crown Prosecution Service and voluntary sector support organisations such as Mencap, BILD, National Autistic Society, and the Down's Syndrome Association. These can all be accessed via the internet, making the job of looking for and finding extra advice and information much easier. You can also join internet discussion groups such as the Choice Forum run by the Foundation for People with Learning Disabilities, which can provide both information and support.

The internet is an invaluable tool for accessing a lot of information, but be careful as not everything on it is correct.

If you don't have access to the internet, a good place to start for additional information on a wide range of local and national topics is your local library. Your employer may also have a specialist library that you should ask your manager about.

Your work setting

If you work for an organisation and are worried about someone you support, then you need to talk to your line manager. They will support you in addressing the issue and will make sure that the organisation's policies and procedures are followed. If you are a personal assistant it may be different as you may not have a structure of policies and procedures to support you, although your contract of employment may have useful information. It may be appropriate for you to talk to the person you support or their family carers to get additional advice and support. In any situation, if you have serious concerns about the person's wellbeing you may need to speak to the adult protection team of your local social services.

If you need additional advice, always discuss safeguarding issues with your line manager or a senior colleague.

If you are concerned about safeguarding and protection issues it is essential that you follow the policies and procedures of your organisation. The book *Principles of Safeguarding and Protection for Learning Disability Workers* in this series gives more information. If you need additional advice, always discuss safeguarding issues with your line manager or a senior colleague.

If the situation you are unhappy with is serious and you feel that action is not being taken, you may need to 'blow the whistle' on your organisation, that is, report your concerns either to the local authority or to the appropriate regulatory authority. In England, this is the Care Quality Commission, in Scotland the Scottish Commission for the Regulation of Care, in Wales the Care and Social Services Inspectorate and in Nothern Ireland the Regulatory and Quality Improvement Authority.

Whistleblowers are protected by law – for more information, go to www.direct.gov.uk

If you feel that your own human rights are being breached, you could talk with your colleagues in the first instance. It may be that you then decide to take the matter up with your line manager or, if you work for a larger organisation, with the human resources department. Alternatively, if the issue involves your manager or how you are managed, it may be more appropriate to speak with your union representative or the Citizens Advice Bureau.

The statutory sector

If it is decided that outside support is needed and the individual concerned is eligible for local authority support from the specialist team for people with learning disabilities, then the person or their family carers or a person from your organisation could contact the individual's social worker or case manager to discuss the situation. If the individual does not have a social worker, at this point they may be referred to one. Depending on the situation and the person's needs, other people who might be able to support include the police, GP or other healthcare workers.

The voluntary sector

Voluntary sector organisations often provide specialist advice and services that you can't access from the statutory services. There are national and local voluntary-sector organisations that support people with learning disabilities and also give information on human rights. Some national organisations also have local groups or branches as well as useful websites, such as Mencap and the National Autistic Society. Many organisations focus specifically on a particular learning disability, such as the Down's Syndrome Association or the Prader-Willi Syndrome Association, and have often been set up by people who have direct family experience of the condition in question. There are also local advocacy groups which support people with learning disabilities to be heard and to live as independent a life as possible. To find information about a local advocacy group, see Chapter 1.

You don't need to go to learning disability specific organisations to get extra information, advice and support; organisations such as your local Citizens Advice Bureau (CAB) can also help. CAB advisers are especially good at signposting – telling people where to go to get appropriate or specialist advice. You might also find the Equality and Human Rights Commission and the British Institute of Human Rights helpful for information on rights and discrimination issues.

Demonstrating actions that model inclusive practice

Modelling inclusive practice is all about 'walking the talk' – it's not enough just to know about equality, diversity and inclusion, you actually have to put the principles into practice. Let's think of modelling inclusive practice as having two connected parts – your own practice and how you respond to other people's practice.

Your own practice

You can assess your practice by working reflectively, always asking yourself if you could have done things differently or better. Your inclusive practice is based on your understanding of and empathy with the person you're supporting and on your thorough knowledge and understanding of human rights. Empathy, or putting yourself in someone else's shoes, is especially important in supporting a person with learning disabilities. The following quote describes support workers failing to work empathetically:

> Especially if there are two carers, they forget about Crystal. That's what was happening very often – Crystal might be sitting on the settee in the middle and they'd be talking across her… And when we said to them no mobile phones, they were just texting, all the time, on their laps.
>
> *Mother and principal carer of Crystal, a young woman with learning disabilities and severe epilepsy*

For more information on reflective practice, the book *Personal Development for Learning Disability Workers* in this series will help you.

Your inclusive practice is also about continually deepening and broadening your knowledge and understanding of the person you're supporting. So for example, in many South Asian cultures it is considered good table manners only to use the right hand when eating, the left hand being used for personal hygiene. If the person you're supporting is from a South Asian background, they may prefer you to use your right hand when supporting them at mealtimes. Equally, of course, the person may have no preference. By having this knowledge – by knowing about the significance of using the right hand and knowing if the individual has a preference – and using it when you provide support to that individual, you are demonstrating inclusive practice.

Thinking point

Think of two things you could do to get to know the person you support better in the next few weeks.

Ways you can get to know the person you support better and develop your inclusive practice are:

- spending time with them and getting to know them better;
- observing their communication closely and developing your communication skills to match how they communicate, finding out if they have a communication passport and reading it;
- reading their person centred plan or support plan (with their permission) and asking if you don't understand something;
- supporting them to pursue interests and take part in activities they enjoy;
- talking to their family and friends about their interests.

How you respond to other people's practice

Inclusive practice is, or should be, part of the way you work, whether that is in a residential home, a day centre or an individual's own home. Responding to other people's practice – whether by questioning, defending or praising it – offers lots of opportunity for modelling inclusive practice. However, typically we don't do these things often enough – we don't question because we don't want to rock the boat, we don't defend because we don't want to get involved and we don't praise because we don't want to appear sentimental or foolish.

Responding to other people's practice can be difficult, especially if you are questioning or challenging it. But it is important for you to understand that doing so is the key to modelling inclusive practice. Questioning or challenging someone else's practice and being open to others doing the same to you is all part of developing an inclusive culture in your work setting.

Other practical ways you can respond to other people's practice are by:

- participating in conversations about equality and rights;
- discussing inclusion and diversity in team meetings and on training days;
- sharing information about legislation and the code of practice when it is appropriate.

By ensuring that human rights, equality and working in an inclusive way are common topics of conversation in your workplace, you are helping to create an environment that promotes them for people with a learning disability.

Demonstrate how to support others to promote equality and rights

As a learning disability worker, there are two main groups of people you can support to promote equality and rights – people with learning disabilities and the family carers, friends and workers who support them.

Supporting people with learning disabilities to understand their rights and about inclusion

This means making sure the individuals you support are always able to communicate as easily and effectively as possible with others – if the person is not communicating as effectively as possible, then they cannot easily understand about equality and rights. You also need to support individuals to know what equality is and what their rights are. This means making sure they have easy access to easy read resources about equality and rights – you could even think about supporting them to build up a small reference section of their own, whether of easy read leaflets and fact sheets or of accessible websites.

If the person is unable to read, you will need to support them to understand about equality and rights using their preferred communication system: this could be using DVD materials or audio files or through drama activities.

Similarly, if the person you support wants to do something specific to promote equality and rights, you need to assist them in any way possible. For example, if they want to make their day service environment more accessible for everyone who attends using signs and symbols, you could support them in all sorts of ways such as printing, laminating or putting the symbols up. Finally, one of the most important ways you can support people with learning disabilities to understand and promote their own equality and rights is to help them access a local advocacy or self-advocacy organisation. Details about how to find a local advocacy organisation can be found at the end of Chapter 1.

Activity

Discuss with your line manager one way that you could support either a person with a learning disability or their family carers to understand their rights.

Supporting colleagues and family members to promote equality and rights

One of the best ways you can do this is by facilitating access to peer support networks so that finding out about and promoting equality and rights becomes a shared activity. For colleagues, you could ask to have this as a regular topic at team meetings or get involved in setting up a monthly peer support group. At such meetings workers can meet up to share best practice, provide mutual support and discuss issues to do with equality and rights – their own as well as those of the individuals they support.

When working with family carers on equality and inclusion issues, you could direct family members to national family carer organisations such as the following:

- Contact a Family at www.cafamily.org.uk

- National Family Carer Network, at www.familycarers.org.uk This organisation specifically supports family carers of adults with a learning disability.

- Carers UK at www.carersuk.org

- The Princess Royal Trust for Carers at www.carers.org

These organisations could offer them support and guidance in promoting equality and rights. Many areas also have local carers' groups; this might be specifically for carers of people with a learning disability or could be open to all carers in an area. You can find out about local groups from your council or local voluntary sector umbrella organisation.

Another good way to support colleagues and family carers is to promote equality and rights by information sharing – taking new knowledge and understanding you have gained and sharing it. If this is not a practice already followed in your team meetings or when you meet family carers, you could consider introducing or promoting it.

Key points from this chapter

Promoting diversity, equality and inclusion in your work setting means:

- finding out about the person as an individual;
- finding out about the local area where the person you're supporting lives.

You may also need to find out about supporting a person:

- of the opposite sex;
- from a different ethnic group;
- from a different cultural background;
- who is younger or older than you;
- who prefers same sex relationships;
- with different religious beliefs or no belief;
- described as having challenging behaviour;
- with a specific learning disability condition or syndrome.

References and where to go for more information

Websites

British Institute of Human Rights www.bihr.org.uk

Carers UK www.carersuk.org

Challenging Behaviour Foundation www.thecbf.org.uk

Community Care www.communitycare.co.uk

Contact a Family www.cafamily.org.uk

Equality and Human Rights Commission www.equalityhumanrights.com

Foundation for People with Learning Disabilities www.learningdisabilities.org.uk

In Control www.in-control.org.uk

Mencap www.mencap.org.uk

National Family Carer Network www.familycarers.org.uk

Personal Assistant Network www.panet.org.uk

The PMLD Network www.pmldnetwork.org

The Princess Royal Trust for Carers www.carers.org

Skills for Care www.skillsforcare.org.uk

Glossary

Advocacy – helping and supporting someone else to speak up for what they want.

Breach – if your human rights are breached, it means they're ignored.

Legislation – the laws that cover a particular area.

Policy – a plan (for a government or an organisation) describing how they will work towards their aims and objectives.

Procedure – a document setting out how something should be done.

Public authorities – organisations like the government, social services, schools and hospitals.

Public services – services which the government provides like social services, hospitals and schools.

Index